The Lemon Shark

BULLIES on the REEF

by Uncle Sid

Illustrations by Sherry A. Mitcham

Xulon Press
2301 Lucien Way #415
Maitland, FL 32751
407.339.4217
www.xulonpress.com

© 2017 by Uncle Sid

All rights reserved solely by the author. The author guarantees all contents are original and do not infringe upon the legal rights of any other person or work. No part of this book may be reproduced in any form without the permission of the author. The views expressed in this book are not necessarily those of the publisher.

Printed in the United States of America.

ISBN: 9781545616796

Fanga was a Lemon Shark.
She was always careful whenever she went out on the reef.

There were always Bullies around like T-Bone, the Tiger Shark, Hacker, the Hammerhead and Bo-Bo, the Bull Shark.
They were always threatening to eat someone or pick on little sharks.

Fanga was in Shark Grade One.
The bullies were in Shark Grade Three.
The shark school officials worked very hard to stop bullying.

After school, sometimes Fanga would hide in a reef fissure until they passed by. But today she was in a hurry because her mom was expecting her new baby brother to be born.

When she passed by the bullies they shouted, "I wonder what Lemon Shark tastes like? Probably very tart!" said T-Bone laughing.

He darted out like he was going to chase her. She quickly dashed home, but decided it was time to tell her parents about the bully sharks.

She told her dad and he called Principal Finn, who said he would call their parents.

Dad had been waiting to take mom to the Shark and Skate Hospital where Sharks and Rays give birth.

The entire Lemon Family was excited to be having a new boy. All the cousins were girls. Dad's brother, Uncle Snipper, was very excited, because he had three girls and no boys.

Later that evening, mom gave birth to a little Lemon boy. He was born with teeth and was a bit yellow. They called him Chops Lemon.

Three months later Chops grew a second row of big teeth right behind the first big row. "This is very unusual," said mom, because the teeth were larger than usual.

When he was one-year-old all his teeth got very big and he was very yellow, even for a Lemon Shark.

"This is very unusual," said dad. "But I like 'em! And, why shouldn't Lemon Sharks be lemony?"

Uncle Snipper came by to see his favorite and only nephew.
"Wow! Those are some big teeth! But I like 'em! It must be a mutation or something! I ain't never seen teeth like this on a Lemon, or a Lemon this lemony!"

"Now, now, Uncle! Calm down!" Fanga giggled. She thought the teeth were cute, too.

"If there is anything sharks respect, it's teeth!" said dad.

When Fanga was going to Shark Grade Seven, Chops was going to Shark Grade One. They were learning about bullying and how not to be afraid, but confident.

Chops noticed all the Shark kids would stare or move over quickly when they swam by, but didn't give it much thought. Chops had teeth almost like a Great White.

Fanga's friend, Snarla, came over. "Hi Fanga! Is this your little brother? He is so cute! What nice teeth he has! And, he is sooo lemony!"

"Oh, he's not that cute!" griped Fanga.

Chops just blushed.

On the way home from school Fanga saw the old bullies waiting under a reef cliff overhang. It was too late to try to dash home!

Bo-Bo the Bull Shark said, "My! What big teeth he has!" T-bone and Hacker laughed! "I wonder if he's as lemony as he looks? Yummy, Yummy!"

Then little Chops swam right up to Bo-Bo and said, "Yeah! And I'm going to chomp you with them!" He wasn't even afraid! "I would hate for you to have to see the Nurse Shark today!"

Hacker responded timidly, "Hey! We were just saying they're big! After all, we like big teeth. No need to get testy! Heh heh!"

T-Bone just looked and didn't say a word. His stripes were even fading.

Chops smiled at him with a really big grin while swimming off slowly and glancing back with one eye. After all, no shark wants to really know what big teeth feel like when they chomp!

Later Chops realized he had taken it too far and decided to tell Principal Finn so there would be no trouble.

The bullies didn't bother Fanga anymore after that. She thought Chops was the best little brother ever! Well, at least sometimes. We know how little brothers can be!

Uncle Sid's real name is Sidney Marlin. He teaches classes on ethics to youth groups in his community and boys and girls clubs and reads to his grandchildren. His Lemon Shark books educate children on the need to use good behavior while teaching on the various life forms in the sea. He can be reached at marlinsid5@gmail.com.

Sherry A. Mitcham
Sherry is a graphic designer and colored pencil artist living in Fayetteville, Georgia with her husband, Bill, and cockerpoo, Chloe. *The Lemon Shark, Bullies on the Reef* is the eighth picture book she has illustrated. She can be reached at samitcham@att.net.

CPSIA information can be obtained
at www.ICGtesting.com
Printed in the USA
BVHW010245031020
590238BV00015B/702